The ALLEGED MEMPHIS SHOOTER HAS BEEN APPREHENDED.

The suspect is Ezekiel Kelly.

Dorothy J. Wheatley

Chapter 1

Chaos

Memphis was put on lockdown for more than two hours on Wednesday after police received a complaint that a man was allegedly driving around shooting at people.

After several hours of commotion, the incident came to an end at around 9:30

p.m. when 19-year-old Ezekiel Kelly was taken into custody in Whitehaven.

After numerous shootings caused terror to spread around the city and a live-streamed video of a guy being shot inside an auto parts store surfaced online, a was caught and detained in Memphis.

The police announced that they had apprehended the suspect on Wednesday night, putting a stop to a spree of shootings in Memphis and a frantic police search for a 19-year-old suspect that effectively shut down Tennessee's second-largest city for five hours.

According to local media, Kelly was injured in a Dodge Challenger crash before being detained by police in Memphis' Whitehaven neighborhood. Before crashing the Dodge, Kelly was seen by police driving a light blue Infiniti, then a gray Toyota with Arkansas license plates. He is a suspect in a vehicle theft that happened at a petrol station in Southaven, a city south of Memphis, according to police.

The authorities advised residents to remain indoors as they started a manhunt at around 4:30 p.m. after the initial shooting.

The Memphis Area Transit Authority has suspended its trolley and bus operations in response to the perceived threat posed by a man who appeared to be driving around the city shooting people at random. The recent kidnapping and murder of a lady who was out on a jog close to campus had already rocked the University of Memphis.

According to the authorities, the individual was responsible for several shootings, some of which may have been recorded on Facebook Live.

Ezekiel Kelly was the man, according to the Memphis Police Department. No charges have been filed against him, but the police described him as "armed and dangerous" while they searched.

The number of persons shot on Wednesday and whether they were random shootings were not immediately known. The authorities have not stated which shootings Mr. Kelly may be associated with, and they did not return calls seeking additional comment.

Around 4:30 p.m. on Wednesday, Memphis Police reported two shootings that took place a minute apart at different locations. According to them, a man was shot and killed instantly on East Parkway South. They reported that a woman was injured in the second shooting on Norris Road close to the southbound Interstate

240 ramp and was sent to a hospital in critical condition.

Police were at four crime locations, including an AutoZone store where the shooter may have live streamed the shooting of a man after entering the store, according to a local TV station.

It was unclear what offence Mr. Kelly was charged with when a first-degree murder warrant was issued for him on Wednesday, according to court documents. He was also charged in 2020 with possessing a firearm, reckless endangerment with a deadly weapon, and two counts of attempted first-degree murder. He was initially charged in juvenile court when he was 17, according to the records, but his case was later moved to adult court. The case's resolution was not immediately obvious. After being tried as an adult, he received a three-year sentence on April 6, 2021, to be served at the Shelby County Department of Corrections.

A payment schedule for the $12,389.50 in penalties and charges that he was required to pay was established.

On March 16, 2022, Kelly, who had been given a three-year term, was freed.

Chapter 2

Opposition of weapons

A shooting has been reported nearby, according to a message sent to University of Memphis students. Nearby Rhodes College, which is 4 miles from the university, instructed both on- and off-campus students to take cover.

Police have not yet released information on the shooting's number of victims or injuries, but the incident comes after nearly two years of increasing gun violence that came with the start of the Covid-19 pandemic. One of more than two dozen states, including Tennessee, has passed laws allowing adults age 21 and older to carry handguns openly or covertly without a permit.

Law enforcement officials opposed the bill because they were concerned that lifting the ban on concealed carry would expose more officers to the risk of being shot.

Chapter 3

Before the shooting, several of his posts

Pictures of Kelly and other young males flaunting large sums of money and weapons can be found on a Facebook page with the handle Zeke Huncho.

On that page, there is a message from August 18 that is addressed to his mother and says, "I swear won't GO without a fight, I promise."

He published a number of older messages on Facebook in the hours before the shootings, including one from 2019 that read: "My home guys turning into bitches, my home females should carry my casket."

In a January 2020 repost, it was written: "I might pray and go sin and then go pray again.

A check of online public records on Wednesday did not yield a phone number for Kelly or anybody connected to him. It was unclear if he had a legal representative who could speak for him.

Facebook's parent firm claimed that it deleted live footage relating to the event, and that it was in contact with Memphis police.

Chapter 4

The shooting spree in Memphis over time

Male discovered deceased in the driveway at 12:56 a.m.

A guy is discovered dead from several gunshot wounds in his car at 4:38 p.m. A dark automobile was seen pulling up next to the victim on video from a nearby business before the shooting.

A female was shot in the leg at 4:40. She is being treated in a hospital in a stable condition.

At 5:59 p.m., the shooter opens fire inside a business while live-streaming on Facebook. A man with a gunshot wound is in the hospital and is in critical condition.

Police are notified at 6:12 p.m. by a concerned citizen that the suspect made threatening comments on Facebook Live.

At 7 o'clock in the evening, Memphis police tweet a warning about a person who is "responsible for many shootings.

7:23 p.m.: A lady is discovered shot to death. According to police, the suspect stole the victim's gray SUV and drove off.

7:24 p.m. Less than half a mile after the first incident, a guy is discovered shot. He is transported to a hospital in a stable condition.

The city of Memphis requests that people stay inside if they do not need to leave.

7:53 p.m.

8:55 p.m.: A woman is discovered shot to death.

In Southaven, Mississippi, at 8:56 p.m., police were called to a carjacking where a Dodge Challenger was seized at gunpoint. The victim has not been hurt. According to authorities, the guy leaves the gray SUV behind and takes off.

Officers start a high-speed chase when they spot the Challenger on Interstate 55 at 8:58 p.m. The culprit is captured by Memphis police and Shelby County Sheriff's Office.

Police said the person is in custody as of 9:26 p.m.

Memphis is experiencing a difficult week, but I have optimism for Memphis, and I am confident that no matter what, United We Stand.

www.ingramcontent.com/pod-product-compliance
Lightning Source LLC
LaVergne TN
LVHW052116160826
845678LV00015B/3579

* 9 7 9 8 3 5 1 6 9 6 3 9 3 *